SPIRITUAL WHOLENESS

THE RETREAT GUIDEBOOK

JANE J. WHITE, M.D.

CONTENTS

Title	v
Information	vii
Purpose	1
Disclaimer	3
Introduction	5
Scripture	7
WORSHIP: Music-Prayer-Journal	9
Worship Assessment	11
Praise and Worship Songs and Hymns	15
Playlist of the Listed Songs	19
Journaling	21
HEALTH: Chronic Diseases	23
Scripture	25
Health Assessment	27
Health Assessment (con't)	31
Stroke	33
Important Information	35
Heart Disease	37
Heart Disease (con't)	39
Cholesterol	41
Cholesterol (con't)	43
Blood Pressure	45
High Blood Pressure	47
Diabetes	49
Diabetes (con't)	51
Diabetes (con't)	53
Cancer	55
Cancer (con't)	57
Mental Health	59
Arthritis	61
Lung Disease	65
Obesity	67
Obesity (con't)	69
Alzheimer's Disease	71

WELLNESS: Nutrition-Physical Fitness-Adequate Sleep	73
Scripture	75
Wellness Definition	77
Important Information	79
Wellness Assessment	81
Lifestyle Assessment	87
Lifestyle Assessment (con't)	89
Lifestyle Assessment Total	91
Lifestyle Assessment (con't)	93
Lifestyle Assessment (con't)	95
Lifestyle Assessment (con't)	97
Lifestyle Assessment (con't)	99
Lifestyle Assessment Total	101
Lifestyle Assessment (con't)	103
Total for sections 4 _____	105
Explanation to Lifestyle Assessment	107
Explanation to Lifestyle Assessment (con't)	109
Primary Guidelines for Healthy Eating	117
Physical Fitness	121
Self-Care for Relaxation and/or Stress Relief	125
Relaxing Teas	129
WEALTH: Giving-Saving-Spending	133
Scripture	135
Mission	137
Introduction	139
Wealth Assessment	141
Giving	145
Saving	147
Spending	149
Budgeting	151
Sample Budget	153
Resources	161
About the Author	163

Spiritual Wholeness Retreat Guidebook
A Guide to Living the Way God Designed
Dr. Jane Julena White

Spiritual Wholeness Retreat Guidebook

A Guide to Living the Way God Designed

Jane J. White, M.D.

Dr. Jane White MD Ministries
Spiritual Wholeness

Dr. White is available to facilitate the Spiritual Wholeness Retreat. Please contact her at JaneWhite55@gmail.com for additional information.

Copyright © 2020 by Jane J. White

All Rights Reserved

Spiritual Wholeness: Retreat Guidebook

Print ISBN: 978-1-7344501-6-3

The Holy Bible, New King James Version (NKJV), Copyright 1982 Thomas Nelson. All rights reserved.

"Worship" Graphic ©Cristian Newsome
"Health" Graphic © Hush Naidoo
"Arthritis" Graphic © CDC
"Lung Disease" Graphic ©Robina Weermeijer
"Cancer" Graphic © National Cancer Institute
"Mental Health" Graphic © Joel Naran
"Obesity" Graphic © i yunmai
"Alzheimer's" Graphic © Cerescan
"Wellness" Graphic © Dan Gold

PURPOSE

THE PURPOSE of the Spiritual Wholeness Retreat is to introduce and/or enhance participants journey to spiritual wholeness and renewal. Spiritual Wholeness is the process of being complete in our relationship with God. It's developing and growing in our worship, health, wellness and wealth.

Worship - fellowship between a person and God.

Health – managing your health

Wellness – the process of living a healthy lifestyle.

Wealth – managing your possessions and resources.

Spiritual wholeness does not make us perfect; however, it does mean we're committed to our quest to being whole. The Spiritual Wholeness Retreat is a great place to begin, renew or enhance your relationship with God.

DISCLAIMER

THIS GUIDEBOOK IS NOT INTENDED as a substitute for the medical advice of physicians. The reader should regularly consult a physician regarding their health and particularly about any symptoms that may require a diagnosis or medical attention.

Although the author has made every effort to ensure the accuracy of information at the time of publishing, the author does not assume and hereby disclaims any liability to any party for any loss, damage, or disruption caused by errors or omission as a result of negligence, accidents, or any other causes.

INTRODUCTION

In the Beginning, God established the way that we should live. However, over time we have gotten away from His prescribed plan. As a result of living life our way, our world has been plagued by busy schedules that has led to unhealthy eating, minimal rest and limited time with God. This in essence has contributed to chronic disease, mental health breakdowns, and frustration.

The Spiritual Wholeness Retreat Manual is designed to equip Retreat Host to help people get back to the foundational plan that God created before the foundation of the earth. Spiritual Wholeness is the process of being complete in four primary areas: *Worship, Health, Wellness* and *Wealth*.

Worship is the process of acknowledging and responding to who God is and what He has done in our lives. There are different ways to worship; however, it primarily involves getting into the presence of God – spending time with Him.

Health – we are affected by various factors like unhealthy diet, genetics, and the environment that can cause chronic diseases and other illnesses. When we are aware of these illnesses, how they affect our bodies and what we can do to improve our conditions, we are striving to live in good health.

Wellness is the process of living well. It includes establishing a health plan that includes eating healthy meals and snacks, maintaining a safe fitness regiment, identifying relaxation methods to help enjoy life as well as getting good proper rest and sleep.

Wealth – managing material possessions and resources with excellence.

SCRIPTURE

*"All the earth shall worship You
And sing praises to You;
They shall sing praises to Your name."*

Selah

Psalm 66:4 NKJV

WORSHIP: MUSIC-PRAYER-JOURNAL

Worship focuses on God and the worshipper decides the process they will take. In our worship experience, we can create an inviting atmosphere through singing praise and worship songs and loving on God. The worshipper may begin by playing worship music and singing alone or sing from their heart to the Lord. This atmosphere allows one to experience God in an intimate way.

Worship through **prayer** involves praying as the Holy Spirit leads. This can be done silently, orally or in tongues. It also creates a space for the worshipper to talk with God and allow God to speak. It's very important that you set time aside (i.e. not rushing) to allow the conversation between you and God to flow uninterrupted.

Worship through **journaling** involves writing down what God spoke to you. You should be as detailed as possible. This allows you to revisit what God spoke and follow any directions He has given.

WORSHIP ASSESSMENT

This assessment was designed to give you a general overview of how you view God and yourself in relation to faith. It also reveals your beliefs about ministry attendance and commitment. This is for your personal knowledge ONLY and can be used to make adjustments where you feel needed.

For each item, please circle the number that best describes your answer according to the scale provided.

1= Strongly Agree 2=Agree 3=Neutral 4=Disagree 5= Strongly Disagree

1. Praying, singing, studying God's word and journaling are all forms of worship.

12345

1. I can worship God in my home at any time.

12345

1. True worship can only be done in a corporate setting.

12345

1. I must pray several times a day for my worship to be effective.

12345

1. God only receives my worship when I pray in tongues.

12345

1. I am not a true worshipper if I don't pray in tongues.

12345

1. I have to have a personal relationship with God to worship.

12345

1. My relationship with God requires me to spend time alone with Him.

12345

1. My relationship with God includes praying, reading and meditating on His word.

12345

1. The Holy Spirit inhabits my worship.

12345

1. I seek God through prayer for wisdom.

12345

1. I challenge myself to learn more about God and His word.

1 2 3 4 5

1. I set aside time each day to connect with God.

1 2 3 4 5

1. I believe it is important to spend time with God each day.

1 2 3 4 5

1. I value my relationship with God above all other relationships in my life.

1 2 3 4 5

1. Prayer includes adoration, thanksgiving, confession, repentance and request.

1 2 3 4 5

1. God speaks to me through His word.

1 2 3 4 5

1. I attend religious services, activities or Bible studies each week.

1 2 3 4 5

1. I pray with intentionality and sincerity.

1 2 3 4 5

1. Journaling allows me to commune with God in an intimate setting.

1 2 3 4 5

GRAND TOTAL_____

Score Between 75 and 100

Good Job

Recommendations: You will need to continue to worship in this way because the Holy Spirit produces this kind of fruit in our lives: love, joy, peace, patience, kindness, goodness, faithfulness, gentleness, and self-control.

Score Between 51 and 74

Room for Improvement

Recommendations: Continue to be a worshiper because, when we make that decision to fix our eyes on Jesus, we quickly realize that God has already begun to release the grip these tendencies can have on our lives.

Score below 50

Need to Rethink Habits

Recommendations: Worship is a declaration of our weakness and God's strength. I challenge you in your next point of need to make that hard choice to be a worshiper and let the breakthrough God fight your battle for you. When we worship, the invisible God is at work doing invisible and powerful things.

PRAISE AND WORSHIP SONGS AND HYMNS

- You Reign — William Murphy
- You Deserve It — Bishop Cortez Vaughnn & JJ Hairston
- You are the Living Word — Fred Hammond & Radical for Christ
- Worth — Anthony Brown & group therAPy
- Won't He Do It — Koryn Hawthorne
- Whom Shall I Fear (God of Angel Armies) — Chris Tomlin
- What You Done — Mali Music
- The Worship Medley — Tye Tribbett
- The Heart of Worship — Passion
- Sweeter — Kim Burrell
- Something about the Name Jesus — Kirk Franklin & Rance Allen
- Praise on the Inside — J Moss
- Our God — Chris Tomlin
- Nobody Greater — VaShawn Mitchell
- Moving Forward — Israel Houghton

- Mighty You Are — The Walls Group
- Love Theory — Kirk Franklin
- Jesus is All — Fred Hammond & Radical for Christ
- It's Working — William Murphy
- Is My Living in Vain?/ You Brought the Sunshine — The Clark Sisters
- Intentional - Travis Greene
- I Need You — Tye Tribbett
- Indescribable — Chris Tomlin
- I Believe — Mali Music
- Hide Me — Kirk Franklin
- Greater is Coming — Jekalyn Carr
- Glorify (Live) — Passion
- Give me a Clean Heart — Fred Hammond & Radical for Christ
- Give Me — Kirk Franklin, Mali Music
- For Your Glory — Tasha Cobbs
- Chains — Kirk Franklin
- Bless the Lord (Son of Man) — Tye Tribbet
- Better is One Day (Live) — Passion & Charlie Hall
- Balm in Gilead — Karen Clark Sheard
- 1 on 1 — Zacardi Cortez

Hymns

- Blessed Assurance
- Come to Jesus
- Come, We that Love the Lord

- God of Grace, God of Glory
- Holy, Holy, Holy
- Love Lifted Me
- Jesus is Calling
- Yes, God is Real.

Taking a photo of the QR Code will lead you to a Spotify

PLAYLIST OF THE LISTED SONGS

PRAYER

Prayer is also a form of worship. It is a conversation between the worshipper and God. The worshipper can create an atmosphere of praise and worship through music or simply begin with prayer. During this part of worship, the worshipper should not do all the talking but make time for God to speak – quieting their spirit so they can hear clearly.

God speaks through different means – a gentle nudge, directs us to a scripture passage, an image, through dreams, and/or visions.

"Then you will call on Me and come and pray to Me, and I will listen to you. You will seek Me and find Me when you seek Me with all your heart." Jeremiah 29:12 - 13

How to Pray.

There are different ways we can pray:

Adorations

Petitions

Thanksgiving

Intercessory

Repentance

There are some who ascribe to the ACTS prayer (adoration, confession, thanksgiving, and supplication). Whatever method you decide to use, know that God hears you when you pray.

Praying God's Word is another process the worshipper can pray. This simply involves prayers that includes Scripture.

For example, a sick person may pray. Dear God, according to the Psalm 107:20 says, *"He sent His Word and healed them and delivered them from their destruction"*; therefore, I am healed.

A person who has more bills than money may pray…Lord, Philippians 4:19 says, *"My God shall supply all of your needs according to your riches in glory through Christ Jesus."* My needs are met according to Your word.

JOURNALING

Journaling as a part of the worship experience is the process of writing down, in as much detail as possible, what God spoke to you in prayer. This allows you to review at a later time as well as serve as reminder of what God spoke to you.

Search the Bible and identify a scripture that relates to what you are dealing with.

God may give a Promise, provide Direction, bring Correction and/or a Challenge. Regardless of how HE speaks you want to journal this special conversation.

Promise – God spoke a specific promise to you. This promise may relate to your personal life, ministry, career, or other areas of your life.

Example: God told you, you were destined to teach. Although you weren't interested in teaching and pursued another career, years later you have an unexplained passion to teach and after making the necessary steps, you become a teacher.

Direction – God is directing you to do something. This may affect you directly, indirectly or may not affect you all. He may be directing you to do something for or on behalf of someone else.

Example: God may direct you to bless a person financially (to meet an immediate need you don't even know they have). This is an opportunity of obedience for you and an opportunity for the person to see faith in action.

Correction – God convicts you, directly or through a specific scripture. This may be in reference to something only you and God know.

Example: God may bring you to a scripture passage during your morning devotion about gossip/slander which brings conviction because you were on the telephone the previous evening talking about a fellow church member.

Challenge – God speaks to you about a personal challenge and/or attack you may be experiencing.

Example: You have experienced betrayal and are contemplating your defense when God, love of forgiveness nudges your remembrance about a sin you were forgiven of and it opens your heart to forgiveness of the person who wronged you.

HEALTH: CHRONIC DISEASES

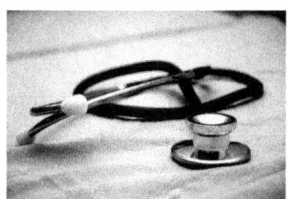

THE FOUNDATION for **healthy living** can be found in the word of God. The Bible clearly gives instructions about our bodies and how to take care of them. While the earth has changed tremendously since our initial guidelines were given, the primary focus is the same.

"For no one ever hated his own flesh, but nourishes and cherishes it, just as Christ also does the church ." Ephesians 5:29

Diet

Eating and maintaining a healthy diet is important. Healthy foods fuel our bodies and provide the energy we need to get through the day.

Water Intake

Our water intake keeps us hydrated and replenishes fluids we lose when we exercise and sweat.

Mind

"Be anxious for nothing, but in everything by prayer and supplication, with thanksgiving, let your requests be made known to God; and the peace of God, which surpasses all understanding, will guard your hearts and minds through Christ Jesus."

Philippians

casting down arguments and every high thing that exalts itself against the knowledge of God, bringing every thought into captivity to the obedience of Christ,

2 Corinthians 10:5

Body

I beseech you therefore, brethren, by the mercies of God, that you present your bodies a living sacrifice, holy, acceptable to God, which is your reasonable service.

Romans 12:1 NKJV

For bodily exercise profits a little, but godliness is profitable for all things, having promise of the life that now is and of that which is to come.

1 Timothy 4:8 English NKJV

SCRIPTURE

"Beloved, I pray that you may prosper in all things and be in health, just as your soul prospers."

III John

HEALTH ASSESSMENT

This assessment was designed to give you a brief overview of how you are managing your health. It will help you review your daily food and beverage intake. It will also help you identify hinderances to caring for your body the way God intended. This is for your personal knowledge ONLY and can be used to make adjustments where you feel needed.

1= Strongly Agree 2=Agree 3=Neutral 4=Disagree 5= Strongly Disagree

1. A person's faith-related beliefs, attitudes and practices can have a positive impact on his or her health.

12345

1. I am open to learning how faith-related beliefs, attitudes and practices might impact in a positive way on my health.

12345

1. My spiritual beliefs affect absolutely every aspect of my life.

12345

1. My thought patterns impact on my emotions, feelings and associated behaviors.

12345

1. I eat a healthy, balanced meal.

12345

1. I drink eight 8 oz. glasses of water a day.

12345

1. I engage in healthy behaviors to care for my body as God's temple.

12345

1. I draw special strength/power from God's Spirit to make informed health decisions.

12345

1. I participate in exercise at least three times a week.

12345

1. I play brain games to keep my mind active.

12345

1. I use my faith to combat anxiety and stress.

12345

1. I exercise at least fifteen minutes a day.

1 2 3 4 5

1. God still heals man from sickness and disease today.

1 2 3 4 5

1. Having a chronic disease means I did something wrong.

1 2 3 4 5

1. Some illnesses are hereditary–related.

1 2 3 4 5

GRAND TOTAL_____

Score Between 0 and 15

Good Job

Recommendations: You will need to make shifts in your food and beverage choices to achieve a healthy pattern and continued vigilance to avoid making wrong food choices and be knowledgeable about family health history.

Score Between 16 and 30

Room for Improvement

Recommendations: You will need to make shifts in your food and beverage choices to achieve a healthy pattern and continued vigilance to avoid making wrong food choices and improve possible lifestyle changes and increase awareness to preventative services.

Score Above 30

Need to Rethink Habits

Recommendations: You will need to make shifts in your food and beverage choices to achieve a healthy pattern and continued vigilance to avoid making wrong food choices, improve possible lifestyle changes and increase awareness to preventative services to avoid chronic diseases and be knowledgeable about family genetics.

HEALTH ASSESSMENT (CON'T)

Health

Chronic diseases are defined broadly as conditions that last 1 year or more and require ongoing medical attention or limit activities of daily living or both. Chronic diseases such as heart disease, cancer, and diabetes are the leading causes of death and disability in the United States. They are also leading drivers of the nation's $3.3 trillion in annual health care costs. – *Centers for Disease Control and Prevention*

Many chronic diseases are caused by a short list of risk behaviors:

- Tobacco use and exposure to secondhand smoke.
- Poor nutrition, including diets low in fruits and vegetables and high in sodium and saturated fats.
- Lack of physical activity.
- Excessive alcohol use.

Who is at risk for chronic disease?

Background risk factors, such as age, sex, level of education and genetic composition.

Behavioral risk factors, such as tobacco use, unhealthy diet and physical inactivity.

Intermediate risk factors, such as elevated blood lipids, diabetes, high blood pressure and overweight/obesity.

1. **Cardiovascular**

A. **Cerebrovascular Disease or stroke**

B. **Heart Disease**

C. **Cholesterol**

D. **High Blood Pressure (Hypertension)**

2. **Diabetes**

3. **Cancer**

4. **Mental Health**

5. **Arthritis**

6. **Lung disease**

7. **Obesity**

8. **Alzheimer's**

STROKE

Description

A stroke happens when a blood clot blocks blood flow to the brain. This causes brain tissue to become damaged or die.

A stroke, sometimes called a brain attack, occurs when something blocks blood supply to part of the brain or when a blood vessel in the brain bursts. In either case, parts of the brain become damaged or die. A stroke can cause lasting brain damage, long-term disability, or even death.

Common Stroke Warning Signs and Symptoms

- Sudden numbness or weakness of the face, arm, or leg—especially on one side of the body.
- Sudden confusion, trouble speaking or understanding.
- Sudden trouble seeing in one or both eyes.
- Sudden trouble walking, dizziness, loss of balance or coordination.
- Sudden severe headache with no known cause.

Risk Factors

- High Blood Pressure
- Bad Cholesterol

- Heart Disorders
- Poor Diet
- Smoking
- Stress
- Depression.
- Lack of Exercise
- Excessive Alcohol usage
- Obesity

NOTE: While these risk factors may contribute to a person having a stroke, having some of these factors does not mean a person will definitely have a stroke. Please talk with your medical provider about your health concerns.

What You Can Do

Up to 80% of strokes could be prevented through healthy lifestyle changes and working with your health care team to control health conditions that raise your risk for stroke. You can help prevent stroke by making healthy lifestyle choices

STROKE

- Eating a healthy diet.
- Maintaining a healthy weight.
- Getting enough physical activity.
- Not Smoking.
- Limiting alcohol use.

For more detailed information go to: www.cdc.gov/stroke/index.htm

IMPORTANT INFORMATION

This information is general and should NOT be used to self-diagnose

HEART DISEASE

Description

The term "heart disease" refers to several types of heart conditions. The most common type of heart disease in the United States is coronary artery disease, which affects the blood flow to the heart. Decreased blood flow can cause a heart attack.

Heart Attack Signs and Symptoms

The five major symptoms of a heart attack are

- Pain or discomfort in the jaw, neck, or back.
- Feeling weak, light-headed, or faint.
- Chest pain or discomfort.
- Pain or discomfort in arms or shoulder.
- Shortness of breath

Other symptoms of a heart attack could include unusual or unexplained tiredness and nausea or vomiting. Women are more likely to have these other symptoms.

Risk Factors

- Family History of Heart Disease
- Inactive Lifestyle
- High Blood Pressure
- Smoking
- Men vs. Women
- Diabetes
- Ethnicity
- Age-Related
- High Blood Cholesterol

NOTE: While these risk factors may contribute to a person having a heart attack, having some of these factors does Not mean a person will definitely have a heart attack. Please talk with your medical provider about your health concerns.

HEART DISEASE (CON'T)

HEART DISEASE

What You Can Do

By living a healthy lifestyle, you can help keep your blood pressure in a healthy range and lower your risk for heart disease and stroke. A healthy lifestyle includes:

- Eating a healthy diet.
- Maintaining a healthy weight.
- Getting enough physical activity.
- Not smoking.
- Limiting alcohol use.

This information is general and should NOT be used to self-diagnose.

CHOLESTEROL

Description

As cholesterol (plaque) builds up in the arteries, the arteries begin to narrow, which lessens or blocks the flow of blood.

Blood cholesterol is a waxy, fat-like substance made by your liver. Blood cholesterol is essential for good health. Your body needs it to perform important jobs, such as making hormones and digesting fatty foods.

Your body makes all the blood cholesterol it needs, which is why experts recommend that people eat as little dietary cholesterol as possible while on a healthy eating plan.

Dietary cholesterol is found in animal foods, including meat, seafood, poultry, eggs, and dairy products.

Strong evidence shows that eating patterns that include less dietary cholesterol are associated with reduced risk of cardiovascular disease, but your overall risk depends on many factors.

Risk Factors.

- Poor Diet.
- Obesity

- Lack of Exercise
- Smoking
- Age
- Diabetes

High Cholesterol ....Mayoclinic.org.Risk factors doesn't indicate illness

What You Can Do

By living a heart healthy lifestyle, you can lower your cholesterol and/or prevent your having high cholesterol.

To prevent high cholesterol

- Eat a low-salt diet that emphasizes fruits, vegetables and whole grains
- Limit the amount of animal fats and use good fats in moderation

CHOLESTEROL (CON'T)

CHOLESTEROL

- Lose extra pounds and maintain a healthy weight.
- Exercise on most days of the week for at least 30 minutes
- Quit smoking
- Drink alcohol in moderation, if at all
- Manage stress

This information is general and should NOT be used to self-diagnose.

BLOOD PRESSURE

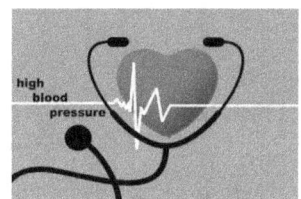

Description

Blood pressure is the force of blood pushing against the walls of your arteries, which carry blood from your heart to other parts of your body. Blood pressure normally rises and falls throughout the day. But if it stays high for a long time, it can damage your heart and lead to health problems. High blood pressure raises your risk for heart disease and stroke, which are leading causes of death in the United States.1

High blood pressure has no warning signs or symptoms, and many people do not know they have it. The only way to know if you have it is to measure your blood pressure. Then you can take steps to control it if it is too high. People with elevated blood pressure levels in between 120/80 and 139/89 mmHg are at high risk for high blood pressure.

Risk Factor

- Age
- Using tobacco
- Race
- Too much salt (sodium) in your diet.
- Family history

- Too little potassium in your diet
- Being overweight or obese
- Drinking too much alcohol.
- Not being physically active
- Stress
- Certain chronic conditions may increase risk of high blood pressure, such as kidney disease, diabetes and sleep apnea.

High blood pressure: Mayoclinic.org

What You Can Do

By living a healthy lifestyle, you can help keep your blood pressure in a healthy range. A healthy lifestyle includes:

- Eating a healthy diet
- Maintaining a healthy weight

HIGH BLOOD PRESSURE

HIGH BLOOD PRESSURE

- Getting enough physical activity
- Not smoking
- Limiting alcohol use
- Control your blood pressure

For more detailed information go to: www.cdc.gov/bloodpressure/about.htm

This information is general and should NOT be used to self-diagnosis

DIABETES

Description

Diabetes is a chronic (long-lasting) disease that affects how your body turns food into energy. There are three main types of diabetes: type 1, type 2, and gestational diabetes (diabetes while pregnant). More than 100 million Americans are living with diabetes (30.3 million) or prediabetes (84.1 million).

Most of the food you eat is broken down into sugar (also called glucose) and released into your bloodstream. When your blood sugar goes up, it signals your pancreas to release insulin. Insulin acts like a key to let the blood sugar into your body's cells for use as energy.

If you have diabetes, your body either doesn't make enough insulin or can't use the insulin it makes as well as it should. When there isn't

enough insulin or cells stop responding to insulin, too much blood sugar stays in your bloodstream. Over time, that can cause serious health problems, such as heart disease, vision loss, and kidney disease. If you have any of the following diabetes symptoms, see your doctor about getting your blood sugar tested:

DIABETES (CON'T)

- Urinate (pee) a lot, often at night
- Are very thirsty
- Lose weight without trying
- Are very hungry
- Have blurry vision
- Have numb or tingling hands or feet
- Feel very tired
- Have very dry skin
- Have sores that heal slowly
- Have more infections than usual

DIABETES (CON'T)

DIABETES

Risk Factors:

- Have prediabetes
- Are overweight
- Are 45 years or older
- Have ever had gestational diabetes (diabetes during pregnancy) or given birth to a baby who weighed more than 9 pounds
- Are African American, Hispanic/Latino American, American Indian, or Alaska Native (some Pacific Islanders and Asian Americans are also at higher risk)
- Have a parent, brother, or sister with type 2 diabetes
- Are physically active less than 3 times a week

What You Can Do

There isn't a cure yet for diabetes, but losing weight (if overweight), eating healthy food, and being active can really help. Taking medicine as needed, getting <u>diabetes self- management education and support</u>, and keeping health care appointments can also reduce the impact of diabetes on your life.

For more detailed information go to:**cdc.org**

This information is eral and should NOT be used to self-diagnose.

CANCER

Description

Cancer is the name given to a collection of related diseases. In all types of cancer, some of A term for diseases in which abnormal cells divide without control and can invade nearby tissues. Cancer cells can also spread to other parts of the body through the blood and lymph systems. There are several main types of cancer. Carcinoma is a cancer that begins in the skin or in tissues that line or cover internal organs. Sarcoma is a cancer that begins in bone, cartilage, fat, muscle, blood vessels, or other connective or supportive tissue. Leukemia is a cancer that starts in blood-forming tissue, such as the bone marrow, and causes large numbers of abnormal blood cells to be produced and enter the blood. Lymphoma and multiple myeloma are cancers that begin in the cells of the immune system. Central nervous system cancers are cancers that begin in the tissues of the brain and spinal cord. Also called malignancy.

Risk Factor

- Age
- Alcohol
- Cancer-Causing Substances
- Chronic Inflammation
- Diet

- Hormones
- Immonosuppression
- Infectious Agents
- Obesity
- Radiation
- Sunlight
- Tobacco

What You Can Do

You can lower your risk of getting cancer by making healthy choices like–

- Avoiding tobacco.
- Protecting your skin.
- Limiting the amount of alcohol, you drink.

CANCER (CON'T)

CANCER

- Keeping a healthy weight.
- Getting tested for hepatitis C.

For more detailed information go to:**cancer.gov**

This information is general and should NOT be used to self-diagnose

MENTAL HEALTH

Description

Mental health is an important part of overall health and well-being. Mental health includes our

Mental health is an important part of overall health and well-being. Mental health includes our emotional, psychological, and social well-being. It affects how we think, feel, and act. It also helps determine how we handle stress, relate to others, and make healthy choices. Mental health is important at every stage of life, from childhood and adolescence through adulthood.

Mental health issues should <u>always</u> be addressed with a licensed medical professional (medical doctor, therapist, psychologist).

Mental health illness is real and in no way, be considered a weakness or lack of faith.

Risk Factor (Categories and examples)

Biophysical

- Family history of Mental Health problems
- Poor nutrition and lack of sleep

Psychological

- Traumatic life experiences
- Low self-esteem, perceived incompetence, negative view of life

Social

- Abused or neglected as a child
- Recent loss by death, divorce or other means

Spiritual

- Perception of being irredeemable or inherently flawed beyond repair
- Conflicting thoughts or doubts surrounding deep religious beliefs

MENTAL HEALTH

What You Can Do

While mental health is complex, preventative measures in the form of self-care and healthy lifestyle choices may help slow the progression of the illness. Maintaining a healthy diet, exercise and development, positive self-regard and building positive and healthy relationships can aid in maintain good mental health. There is a comprehensive list of problems that comes from the Diagnostic Service Manual or DSM. To learn a basic overview and access a link for more detailed information go to:**americanmentalwellness.org**

This information is general and should NOT be used to self-diagnose.

ARTHRITIS

Description

Arthritis means inflammation or swelling of one or more joints. It describes more than 100 Arthritis means inflammation or swelling of one or more joints. It describes more than 100 conditions that affect the joints, tissues around the joint, and other connective tissues. Specific symptoms vary depending on the type of arthritis, but usually include joint pain and stiffness.

Risk Factor

Non-modifiable risk factors are risk factors that you cannot control. These include:

- Age
- Sex
- Genetics

Modifiable risk factors are risk factors that you can control. Making lifestyle changes can decrease your risk of getting some types of arthritis or making arthritis worse.

- Overweight/Obesity

- Physical inactivity
- Joint injuries
- Smoking
- Infection
- Occupation
- Diet

What You Can Do

There are no known preventative measures against arthritis; however, managing the modifiable factors can significantly lower risk.

- Healthy eating
- Weight loss
- Exercise when possible
- Stop smoking

For more detailed information go to: **arthritis.ca**

This information is general and should NOT be used to self-diagnose

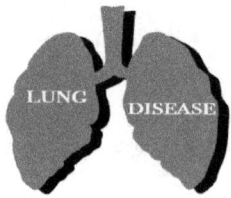

Description

Lung disease refers to any disease or disorder in which the lungs do not function properly. Lung disease is the third leading killer in the United States, responsible for one in seven deaths, and is the leading cause of death among infants under the age of one. Some lung diseases, like asthma and emphysema, involve a narrowing or blockage of the airways resulting in poor air flow. Others, including pulmonary fibrosis, pneumonia and lung cancer, are caused by a loss of elasticity in the lungs that produces a decrease in the total volume of air that the lungs can hold. Research has shown that long-term exposure to air pollutants can reduce lung growth and development and increase the risk of developing asthma, emphysema, and other respiratory diseases. Results from the NIEHS-supported Harvard Six Cities Study, the largest available database on the health effects of outdoor and indoor air pollution, show a strong association between exposure to ozone, fine particles and sulfur dioxide, and an increase in respiratory symptoms, reduced lung capacity, and risk of early death.

Risk Factor

- Tobacco products/Smokeless products/Electronic cigarettes/Second hand smoke
- Family history
- Exposure to inflammatory pollutants
- Some auto immune disease

LUNG DISEASE

LUNG DISEASE

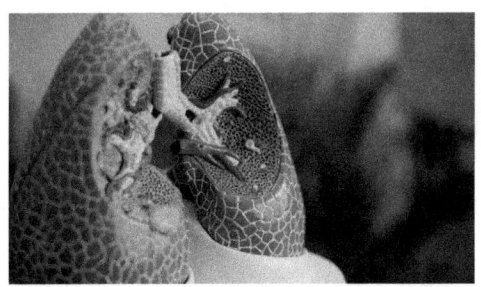

What You Can Do

- Don't smoke or quit smoking
- Try to avoid secondhand smoke
- Reduce exposure to pollutants

www.cdc.gov/tobacco/basic_information/health_effects/index.htm

This information is general and should NOT be used to self-diagnose.

OBESITY

Description

Obesity is a complex health disorder that affects both adults and children. Childhood obesity is a serious problem in the United States. Obesity means having too much body fat. Obesity occurs over time when a person eats more calories than they can use.

Being obese puts people at risk for many health problems. The more body fat a person has and the more they weigh, the more likely they are to develop diseases such as diabetes, heart disease, stroke, arthritis, breathing problems, and some cancers.

Body Mass Index (BMI) is a person's weight in kilograms divided by the square of height in meters. A high BMI can be an indicator of high body fatness. To calculate BMI, see the Adult BMI Calculator or determine BMI by finding your height and weight in this. If your BMI is less than 18.5, it falls within the underweight range.

- If your BMI is 18.5 to <25, it falls within the normal.
- If your BMI is 25.0 to <30, it falls within the overweight range.
- If your BMI is 30.0 or higher, it falls within the obese range.

Risk Factor

- Environment
- Family history and genetics
- Metabolism
- Behavior or habits

OBESITY (CON'T)

OBESITY

What You Can Do

- Weight loss can improve or prevent many of the health problems
- Dietary changes
- Increased physical activity and behavior changes

For more information go to: www.cdc.obesity/data/adult.htm

This information is general and should NOT be used to self-diagnose.

ALZHEIMER'S DISEASE

Description

What is Alzheimer's Disease?

- The most common type of dementia.
- A progressive disease beginning with mild memory loss possibly leading to loss of the ability to carry on a conversation and respond to the environment.
- Involves parts of the brain that control thought, memory, and language.
- Can seriously affect a person's ability to carry out daily activities.

Although scientists are learning more every day, right now, they still do not know what causes Alzheimer's disease. There probably is not one single cause, but several factors that affect each person differently such as:

Risk Factor

- Age
- Family history
- Genetics
- Head injury
- Ethnicity

What You Can Do

Preventative studies have shown that the following list can help lower Risk of Alzheimer's:

- Regular exercise
- Healthy diet
- Maintain healthy social connections and intellectual activity.

For more detailed information go to: www.cdc,gov/aging/caregiving/index.htm

This information is general and should NOT be used to self-diagnose.

WELLNESS: NUTRITION-PHYSICAL FITNESS-ADEQUATE SLEEP

SCRIPTURE

Therefore, I urge you, brothers and sisters, in view of God's mercy, to offer your bodies as a living sacrifice, holy and pleasing to God – this is your true and proper worship.

Romans 12:1 NIV

WELLNESS DEFINITION

Wellness is the quality or state of being in good health especially as an actively sought goal. *Merriam*-Webster Dictionary

It includes healthy eating, physical fitness, and adequate sleep. When one of these is lacking, it affects us mentally, physically and spiritually.

Wellness is a necessity especially if we want to maneuver life's busy schedules in excellence.

The way we treat our bodies when we are younger, often affects how our bodies treat us when we are older. Yet, despite the early lack of attention we may give ourselves in this fast-paced world, we can always make changes and commit to living healthier.

Nutrition

Think about what motivates you to eat healthier. Do you want to look better? Feel better? Lose weight? Increase your energy level?

Physical Fitness

Regular exercise is important to wellness. Establishing a healthy exercise regimen can increase your stamina. Regular exercise is important to the state of good health and strength achieved through exercise

NOTE: Always consult with your primary care physician before beginning an exercise regimen.

Adequate Sleep

Adequate sleep can help reduce your risk of some chronic diseases and your chances of being involved in sleep-related accidents. Adequate sleep also recharges your body and mind. Keep getting your zzzz's.

When you make the commitment to engage in healthy eating, physical fitness and getting adequate sleep, you are creating a successful wellness plan.

IMPORTANT INFORMATION

NOTE: (This section must be facilitated by persons with certifications in the specified area of information).

WELLNESS ASSESSMENT

"for no one ever hated his own flesh, but nourishes and cherishes it, just as Christ also does the church." Ephesians 5:29

Healthy Eating

In a typical day, how many servings do you have of the following?

Fruits

Examples of one serving include one small apple, ½ cup sliced pear, 1 cup blueberries, grapes, cubed melon, or two pineapple rings.

Cups 1 2 2 ½ 3 4+

Vegetables

Examples of one serving include 1 cup cooked or raw broccoli, or cauliflower or 2 cups green leafy vegetables.

Cups 1 2 2 ½ 3 4+

Whole grains

Examples of one serving include one slice of whole-grain bread, ½ cup whole-grain cereal, ½ cup cooked whole-wheat pasta or one small whole-grain muffin.

Ounces 1 2 ½ 3 4 5+

Dairy

Examples of one serving is 6-ounce portion of fat-free yogurt is equal to ¾ Cup-equivalent dairy, or 1½ ounces portion of cheddar cheese is equal to 1 cup-

equivalent dairy.

Ounces 1 2 ½ 3 4 5+

Protein

Examples of one serving is 1 large egg is equal to 1 ounce-equivalents protein foods, 2 tablespoons of peanut butter is equal to 2 ounce-equivalents protein foods, 1-ounce portion of walnuts is equal to 2 ounce-equivalents protein foods,

½ Cup portion of black beans is equal to 2 ounce-equivalents protein foods and

4 ounce portion of pork is equal to 4 ounce-equivalents protein foods.

Ounces 1 2 ½ 3 4 5+

Fitness

In a typical week, how many days do you do moderate-intensity activities that increase your heart rate but aren't exhausting. Examples may include brisk walking, bicycling, low-impact swimming and dancing.

- None
- 1 day
- 2 days
- 3 days
- 4 days
- 5 days

- 6 days
- 7 days

Stress and resilience (physical activity, meditating, achieving balance).

Physical activity

- None
- 1 day
- 2 days
- 3 days
- 4 days
- 5 days
- 6 days
- 7 days

Meditating

- 1 day
- 2 days
- 3 days
- 4 days
- 5 days
- 6 days
- 7 days

Focusing on achieving balance in your life

- 1 day
- 2 days
- 3 days
- 4 days
- 5 days
- 6 days
- 7 days

Sleep

Do you get adequate sleep each night? How many hours?

- 3 hours
- 4 hours
- 5 hours
- 6 hours
- 7 hours
- 8 hours

GRAND TOTAL_____

Score Between 42 and 52

Good Job

Recommendations: You will need to continue with achieving a healthy eating patterns and continued vigilance on choices that will affect your eating behavior, fitness, meditation, stress, sleep and balance.

Score Between 28 and 41

Room for Improvement

Recommendations: You will need to strive more to achieve a healthy eating pattern and keep a vigilant eye on your lifestyle to avoid making wrong choices that will affect your eating behavior, fitness, meditation, stress, sleep and balance in your life.

Score Below 28

Need to Rethink Habits

Recommendations: You must immediately start eating healthy and put balance in your life by getting a checkup and to work on fitness, meditation, stress level and sleep to avoid developing a chronic disease.

LIFESTYLE ASSESSMENT

Lifestyle Assessment: What is your Chemical, Environmental and Contaminant Exposure?

Fill out this assessment to see how you score.

Rate each of the following from 0 to 3. If it does not apply, put a 0. few times a month = 1 weekly = 2 daily or almost daily = 3

Section One – Do you:

CHEMICALS SWALLOWED

LIFESTYLE ASSESSMENT (CON'T)

1. ___ Eat at a restaurant:
2. ___ Eat fast food
3. ___ Prepare/eat boxed meals
4. ___ Eat frozen meals
5. ___ Eat canned soups
6. ___ Know about chemicals on fruits/vegetable
7. ___ use margarine or other types of processed spreads

1. ___ cook with vegetable oils
2. ___ eat microwaved popcorn
3. ___ drink carbonated drinks
4. ___ drink diet drinks
5. ___ use artificial sweeteners
6. ___ drink flavored drinks with food colorings
7. ___ eat candy with food colorings
8. ___ use plastic containers to store food

LIFESTYLE ASSESSMENT TOTAL

Total for section 1 _____

LIFESTYLE ASSESSMENT (CON'T)

Section Two-Do you or have you:

CHEMICALS ABSORBED

LIFESTYLE ASSESSMENT (CON'T)

1. ___ take any prescription medications
2. ___ smoke inside home/office
3. ___ use perfume or cologne
4. ___ wear cosmetics
5. ___ color, perm, or straighten your hair
6. ___ use antibacterial soaps
7. ___ use bleach (chlorine) in your laundry or for cleaning

1. ___ use ammonia for cleaning
2. ___ use scented laundry detergent softeners, or dryer sheets
3. ___ use powdered, liquid, or foam scrubbing solutions or cleansers in your household

1. ___ use air fresheners
2. ___ burn candles in your home or office
3. ___ use mothballs in your home
4. ___ use wood to heat your home
5. ___ been exposed to smog
6. ___ park your vehicle in a garage attached to your home

LIFESTYLE ASSESSMENT (CON'T)

Total for sections 2

Section Three- Do you use, develop or were you exposed to:

CONTAMINANT EXPOSURE

LIFESTYLE ASSESSMENT (CON'T)

1. ___ pesticides
2. ___ lead (home built during 1979-2005)
3. ___ arsenic
4. ___ nitrates and nitrites
5. ___ rodenticides
6. ___ herbicides
7. ___ Fungicides
8. ___ paints and paint thinners
9. ___ wood preservatives or stains
10. ___ alloys (e.g., jewelry making)
11. ___ dyes (e.g., textile

LIFESTYLE ASSESSMENT TOTAL

Total for section 3___

LIFESTYLE ASSESSMENT (CON'T)

Section Four-Do you have or have you:

ENVIRONMENTAL EXPOSURE

1. ___ worked in a mine
2. ___ silver amalgam fillings in your teeth
3. ___ tattoos with colored ink
4. ___ receive flu shots or other vaccinations
5. ___ any other type of metal in your mouth
6. ___ currently smoke cigarettes
7. ___ smoked cigarettes before
8. ___ been exposed to secondhand smoke
9. ___ water damage, damp or mildew smell at home, work, school, or car

1. ___ develop symptoms when you smell perfume, cologne, or strong odors

1. ___ Drink 8 oz of water

TOTAL FOR SECTIONS 4 _____

GRAND TOTAL_____

Score Between 0 and 15

Good Job

Recommendations: You will need to make shifts in your food and beverage choices to achieve a healthy pattern and continued vigilance to avoid chemical exposure

Score Between 16 and 30

Room for Improvement

Recommendations: You will need to make shifts in your food and beverage choices to achieve a healthy pattern and continued vigilance to avoid chemical exposure possible lifestyle changes, and increasing awareness to avoid chemical exposure

Score Above 30

Need to Rethink Habits

Recommendations: You will need to make shifts in your food and beverage choices to achieve a healthy pattern and continued vigilance to avoid chemical exposure and possible lifestyle changes with increasing awareness to avoid chemical exposure.

Developed by Dr. Jane White

EXPLANATION TO LIFESTYLE ASSESSMENT

Explanation to Lifestyle Assessment

Section One- Do you:

1. Eat at a restaurant - Portion size too big and High fat meals
2. Eat fast food - Consuming too much sugar, carbohydrates and fats exceeds that requirement and is bad for the health
3. Prepare/eat boxed meals – Portion size, extra preservative and low in nutrients (higher in salt and freezing method)
4. Eat frozen meals – Blanching to preserve color of vegetables causes decrease in nutrient value
5. Eat canned soups - While processing may remove some of the nutrients, such as water soluble-vitamins, other nutrients, such as fiber
6. Know about chemicals on fruits/vegetables - Detectable residues of organophosphate pesticides has been detected.
7. Use margarine or other types of processed spreads – Artery clogging and trans-fat, so the healthiest choice is to skip both and use liquid oils, such as olive, canola and safflower oil, instead.
8. Cook with vegetable oils – Releases toxic chemicals linked to cancer and other diseases
9. Eat microwaved popcorn – Bag lined with perfluorooctanoic acid, when heated has been linked to infertility & cancer

10. Drink carbonated drinks - Regular consumption of sugary drinks is linked to numerous health problems including diabetes, heart disease, asthma, COPD and obesity.
11. Diet drinks - Artificial sweeteners and drinking high amounts of diet soda is associated with an increased risk of obesity and metabolic syndrome
12. Use artificial sweeteners - You are replacing sugars with chemicals when choosing artificial sweeteners.
13. Drink flavored drinks with food colorings - Food dyes can cause everything from hyperactivity and allergic reactions to cancer
14. Eat candy with food colorings – Contain plenty of chemical linked to brain tumors, cancers and mild allergic reactions
15. Use plastic containers to store food - All plastics leach chemicals into our food, and the FDA has admitted this

EXPLANATION TO LIFESTYLE ASSESSMENT (CON'T)

Section Two-Do you or have you:

1. Take any prescription medications – Many side effects, we trust FDA to make sure that our medicine is safe and effective, but it is also imperative that we each do our own research based on our individual needs and circumstances
2. Smoke inside home/office - Exposure to several of the main chemical components found in tobacco smoke
3. Use perfume or cologne - Perfume has the highest and strongest concentration of oils to alcohol, while cologne is more diluted with more alcohol and does dry out the skin. Contact with certain oils might not be safe.
4. Wear cosmetics - Preservatives are chemicals added to the cosmetic to prolong its shelf life and inhibit bacterial growth. Some examples of include such as Paraben, Imidazolidinyl urea, Quaternium-15, DMDM hydantoin, Phenoxyethanol, Formaldehyde. Choose "preservative free" and "fragrance free" products when shopping.
5. Color, perm, or straighten your hair - Any chemical treatment that changes the pattern of your hair will take its toll.
6. Use antibacterial soaps - Antibacterial soaps are no more effective than regular soap and water for killing disease-causing germs,

according to the CDC/FDA. You Can Skip It, Use Plain Soap and Water

7. Use bleach (chlorine) in your laundry or for cleaning - This product is very corrosive, meaning that it could corrode the skin and leave it very irritated. When consumed or smelt, the chemicals can cause respiratory problems like Asthma.
8. Use ammonia for cleaning - The key to using the ammonia safely is to have it properly diluted. Exposure to high concentrations of ammonia in air causes immediate burning of the eyes, nose, throat and respiratory tract and can result in blindness, lung damage or death.
9. Use scented laundry detergent softeners, or dryer sheets - Quaternary ammonium compounds (Quats) can provoke allergic reactions and can also cause skin and respiratory problems. Fragrances can contain numerous compounds that can provoke allergic reactions, unscented products will work.
10. Use powdered, liquid, or foam scrubbing solutions or cleansers in your household - But while the chemicals in cleaners foam, bleach, and disinfect to make our dishes, bathtubs and countertops gleaming and germ-free, many also contribute to indoor air pollution, are poisonous if ingested, and can be harmful if inhaled or touched. In fact, some cleaners are among the most toxic products found in the home.
11. Use air fresheners - Contain variable quantities of phthalates. Phthalates are added to air fresheners because they help dissolve and transport fragrances. These chemicals are also found in makeup, paint and nail polish. Have been linked to cancer, decreased testosterone and lowered sperm counts
12. Burn candles in your home or office - Paraffin wax is made from petroleum, while soy or other vegetable-based waxes and beeswax aren't. Inhaling the pollutants drifting into the air from the candle can contribute to the development of common allergies or cancer.
13. Use mothballs in your home - Mothballs can seriously impair indoor air quality. Mothballs are a pesticide product that contain either naphthalene or paradichlorobenzene as active ingredients. Both chemicals are toxic fumigants (which means they volatilize into the air).

14. Use wood to heat your home - When wood burns, it releases hazardous gases (e.g., nitrogen oxide and carbon monoxide) and soot (particulate matter).
15. Been exposed to smog – When exercising in a polluted environment for more than 15 minutes, the positive impact of activity will gradually be offset by the negative impact of air pollution.
16. Park your vehicle in a garage attached to your home - Health issues if you do not properly insulate and ventilate your garage and if you store any potentially hazardous materials inside it. Carbon monoxide gas and oil fumes can infiltrate your home from your garage if you are not careful.

Section Three- Do you use, develop or were you exposed to:

1. Pesticides - Pesticides and other foreign substances in food products and drinking water along with toxic pollutants in the air pose an immediate threat to human health, whereas other contaminants gradually build up in the environment and in the human body, causing disease long after first exposure
2. Lead (homes built during 1979) - Lead exposure can have serious consequences for the health of children. At high levels of exposure, lead attacks the brain and central nervous system to cause coma, convulsions and even death. There is no known safe blood lead concentration
3. Arsenic - Natural medicines can be contaminated with arsenic and may produce symptoms of poisoning when consumed in large amounts or for extended periods of time. Cases of arsenic poisoning have been reported with homeopathic arsenic products and with kelp supplements.
4. Nitrates or Nitrites - Without additives like nitrites, the meat would turn brown very quickly. Bottom Line: Nitrates and Nitrites are compounds consisting of Nitrogen and Oxygen atoms. Nitrates can turn into Nitrites, which can then form either Nitric Oxide (good) or Nitrosamines (bad). We do know that consuming processed meats is strongly linked to an increased risk of cancer in the digestive tract,

and many people believe that the nitrates/nitrites are the reason for that.
5. Rodenticides - Rodenticides are pesticides that kill rodents. Rodents include not only rats and mice, but also squirrels, woodchucks, chipmunks, porcupines, nutria, and beavers. They can damage crops, violate housing codes, transmit disease, and in some cases cause ecological damage.
6. Herbicides - It is illegal to use herbicides in any manner inconsistent with its labeling. It can pose health dangers for anyone exposed to these chemicals and have been linked to non-Hodgkin lymphoma and birth defects. Most of the time, natural, organic herbicides have no adverse effects. Some non-toxic substances to remove weeds include, clove oil, vinegar, cinnamon oil, lemon juice and corn gluten.
7. Fungicides - A fungicide is a type of pesticide used to kill fungal pathogens on plants. Viruses, nematodes and bacteria also cause plant diseases. Some fungicides can irritate skin and eyes, while others may cause throat irritation and coughing when inhaled.
8. Paints and paint thinners - Important sources of environmental contamination include mining, smelting, manufacturing and recycling activities, and, in some countries, the continued use of leaded paint, leaded gasoline, and leaded aviation fuel.
9. Wood preservatives or stains - Treated with chemicals for protection, it can be hazardous when not handled correctly. If the wood is burned, trimmed, or cut, it can release harmful toxins into the air. Pressure-treated wood should not be used for gardens or come in frequent contact with food and water.
10. Alloys (e.g., jewelry making)- Most common type of material used for jewelry is Brass and is made from copper and zinc (mixed of 2 alloy mental) causes skin allergies.
11. Dyes (e.g., textile) - Most natural dyes are mordant dyes particularly those in the hard metal category, can be hazardous to health and extreme care must be taken in using them.

Section Four-Do you have or have you:

1. Worked in a mine - Coal miners are also at risk of developing chronic

respiratory illnesses, which are caused by breathing in thick coal dust. Black lung disease is a common respiratory illness contracted by coal miners.

2. Silver amalgam fillings in your teeth - They're also known as 'mercury fillings 'because – you guessed it – there is mercury in amalgam fillings. It's this ingredient which has made dental amalgam the subject of continuing controversy, due to concerns about its impact on human health both directly and through environmental pollution.

3. Tattoos with colored ink - Tattoos breach the skin, which means that skin infections and other complications are possible, including: Allergic reactions (Tattoo dyes), Skin infections (granuloma can form around tattoo ink), Bloodborne diseases (equipment contaminated with infected blood), MRI complications (tattoo pigments can interfere with the quality of the image).

4. Receive flu shots or other vaccinations - Receiving the flu vaccine is a very effective way to prevent yourself and your family from developing the flu. There are many benefits to influenza vaccination, as well as some associated risks.

5. Any other type of metal in your mouth – The safest and best material that a dentist can put in your mouth is 24-karat gold. Grade-1 titanium or zirconia (in certain cases).

6. Currently smoke cigarettes - Every cigarette that you smoke takes away seven minutes of your lifetime. But if you do the math it adds up like it's black tar that builds up in your lungs and can cause 12 different kinds of cancers throughout your body.

7. Smoked cigarettes before - People who stop smoking greatly reduce their risk for disease and early death. You are never in the clear of COPD. It depends very much on how much you smoked. So, if you smoked, you know, one cigarette a day for maybe a year, probably your risk is very little. But if you smoked a pack a day for 20 years, then 20 to 30 years later you are still at risk.

8. Been exposed to secondhand smoke - Can lead to increased risk to emphysema, cardiovascular disorders and respiratory problems. Secondhand smoke is a health risk with a negative impact to the people around you and can cause anyone around you to procure

cancer as well. One of the leading causes of deaths and health concerns in the world.

9. Water damage, damp or mildew smell at home, work, school, or car – There are certain types of molds that produce what are called mycotoxins. These molds are particularly dangerous and create a toxic breathing environment for you, your children and your pets. breathing in large amounts of these mycotoxins can impair the entire human system and can even lead to death.
10. Develop symptoms when you smell perfume, cologne, or strong odors - If you sneeze every time you get a whiff of perfume or room deodorizer, you may be one of millions of people with a fragrance sensitivity or an allergy to some chemical in the perfume/cologne/strong odors.
11. Drink 8 oz of water - Your body weight is made up of 60 percent water. Every system in your body needs water to function. Ages 19 and older is around 131 ounces for men and 95 ounces for women. This refers to your overall fluid intake per day, including anything you eat or drink that contains water, like fruits or vegetables. Of this total, men should get around 13 cups from beverages. For women, it's 9 cups.

https://www.fda.gov/forconsumers/consumerupdates/ucm378393.htm

https://www.healthline.com/health/beauty-skin-care/how-long-does-a-perm-last#other-fa-qs

https://www.symptomfind.com/web

https://www.ehow.com/list_6728811_disadvantages-air-freshener.html

https://www.organicconsumers.org/news/how-toxic-are-your-household-cleaning-supplies

https://www.chicagotribune.com/lifestyles/home-and-garden/sc-cons-1204-savvy-candles-20141201-story.html

https://blogs.webmd.com/from-our-archives/20110222/are-mothballs-safe

https://www.ncbi.nlm.nih.gov/pmc/articles/PMC5606636/

https://www.who.int/news-room/fact-sheets/detail/lead-poisoning-and-health

https://www.webmd.com/vitamins/ai/ingredientmono-1226/arsenic

https://www.healthline.com/nutrition/are-nitrates-and-nitrites-harmful

https://www.npic.orst.edu/factsheets/rodenticides.html

https://www.abchomeandcommercial.com/blog/herbicide-pros-cons/

https://homeguides.sfgate.com/fungicide-dangers-84709.html

www.designbuildersmd.com/blog/what-are-the-advantages-and-disadvantages-of-pressure-treated-wood-decks

https://www.gvcoj.com/blogs/news/lesson-4-pros-and-cons-of-metals-commonly-used-in-fashion-jewelry

https://www.wisegeek.com/what-are-the-pros-and-cons-of-working-as-a-coal-miner.htm

https://www.dentaly.org/en/tooth-filling/amalgam-fillings/

https://www.mayoclinic.org/tattoos-and-piercings/art-20045067/in-depth/art-20045067

https://www.healthline.com/health/flu-shot-pros-and-cons#takeaway

https://straightupdoc.com/?p=158

https://longevity.media/the-cons-of-smoking-cigarettes-for-smokers

https://www.verywellmind.com/the-pros-and-cons-of-smoking-2824462

https://www.cdc.gov/tobacco/data_statistics/fact_sheets/cessation/quitting/index.htm

https://www.globalhealingcenter.com/natural-health/dangers-of-mold/

https://www.everydayhealth.com/allergies/fragrance-sensitivity.aspx

https://www.healthline.com/health/how-much-water-should-I-drink - recommendations

Developed by Dr. Jane White

PRIMARY GUIDELINES FOR HEALTHY EATING

Primary Guidelines for Healthy Eating

Here are **five** primary guidelines that encourage healthy eating lifestyles. These guidelines may require individuals to make changes in their food and beverage choices to achieve a healthy eating plan. However, an adaptable framework in which individuals can enjoy foods that meet their personal, cultural, and traditional preferences can be achieved and fit within one's budget.

1. Follow a healthy eating diet throughout your life. All food and beverage choices are important. Choose a healthy eating pattern with an appropriate calorie level to help achieve and maintain a healthy body weight, support nutrient adequacy, and reduce the risk of chronic disease.
2. Focus on variety in your diet: nutrient enrichment and calorie intake. Choose nutrient-rich foods from each food group in recommended amounts.
3. Limit calories from added sugars and saturated fats and reduce sodium intake. Adopt dietary restrictions such as, low in added sugars, saturated fats, and sodium. Reduce foods and beverages higher in these components to amounts that fit within healthy eating patterns.
4. Make wiser decisions regarding healthier food and beverage choices. Choose nutrient-rich foods and beverages from all food groups in

place of less healthy choices. Consider cultural and personal preferences to make these changes easier to accomplish and maintain.
5. Support healthy eating lifestyles.

A healthy diet includes:

• A variety of vegetables from all the subgroups—dark green, red and orange, legumes (beans and peas), starchy, and other

• Fruits, especially whole fruits

• Grains, at least half of which are whole grains

• Fat-free or low-fat dairy, including milk, yogurt, cheese, and/or fortified soy beverages

• A variety of protein foods, including seafood, lean meats and poultry, eggs, legumes (beans and peas), and nuts, seeds, and soy products

• Oils A healthy eating pattern limits:

Saturated fats and trans fats, added sugars, and sodium

• Daily calorie intake – less than 10 percent of from added sugars

• Daily calorie intake – less than 10 percent of from saturated fats

• Daily intake – less than 2,300 milligrams (mg) per day of sodium

• If alcohol is consumed, it should be consumed in moderation—up to one drink per day for adult women and up to two drinks per day for adult men

  • In addition to the above guidelines, physical activity helps promote health and reduce the risk of chronic disease. Everyone should aim to achieve and maintain a healthy body weight. The relationship between diet and physical activity contributes to calorie balance and managing body weight. Adults need a minimum of 2 ½ hours of moderate intensive physical activity two or more days each week. Youth ages 6 to 17 years old need at least 60 minutes of physical activity per day, including aerobic, muscle-strengthening, and bone-strengthening activities. Beginning and maintaining regular physical activity can provide many health benefits. Statistics indicate that regular exercise helps people maintain a healthy weight, prevent excessive weight gain, and lose weight when combined with a healthy, low calorie diet. Additionally, regular physical activity lowers the risk of early death, coronary heart disease, stroke, high blood pressure, adverse blood lipid profile, type 2 diabetes, breast and colon cancer, and metabolic syndrome; it also reduces depression and prevents falls. Most people maintain a consistent physical regiment when participating in activities they enjoy.

Developed by Dr. Jane J. White

Nutrition Guide available as a pdf by contacting Dr. Jane White at janewhite55@gmail.com.

PHYSICAL FITNESS

Physical Fitness

Please check with your Physicians before beginning any Physical Fitness regimen.

Relaxation Techniques

Identifying an outlet for stress and/or anxiety management is an important part of living a holistically healthy lifestyle. Physical activity may contribute to increased relaxation as well as weight loss. In addition, physical activity causes endorphins to be released in the brain, having positive effects on the body.

Scan QR Code (with camera or QR code reader) to view Relaxation Techniques videos.

Relaxation Exercises

Physical activity is essential to a holistically healthy life. No matter how active you are, there's always something else you can do to stay fit.

Scan QR Code (with camera or QR code reader) to view Relaxation Exercises video.

Information attained from the American Psychological Association, the Anxiety and Depression Association, and the Harvard Health Publishing.

SELF-CARE FOR RELAXATION AND/OR STRESS RELIEF

Self-Care for Relaxation and/or Stress Relief

Self-care involves

Stress relievers such as regular physical activity, meditating, and focusing on achieving balance in your life often produce good health results. Essential oils, healthy drinks and teas as well as good skin care can also be used to relax or relieve stress.

Essential Oils

Essential oils can be used to help you relax (releasing stress); increase energy levels and produce an atmosphere of calmness (oil diffusers). If you're having trouble handling stress on your own, talk with your Primary Care Physician.

Scan QR Code (with camera or QR code reader) to view Essential Oils video.

Relaxing Drinks

Family gatherings, game nights with friends, a relaxing afternoon alone reading, and the many other ways people enjoy life can be enhanced by a healthy drink. Whether it's a smoothie to start your day, or an infused refreshing drink at a weekend gathering, healthy drinks are a great way to make an event special.

Scan QR Code (with camera or QR code reader) to view Relaxing Drinks video.

Self-Care for Relaxation and/or Stress Relief 127

RELAXING TEAS

Relaxing Teas

There are many challenges people face each day that causes stress and overwhelming feelings. This can sometimes disrupt a person's productivity.

There are herbal teas that can help reduce stress and promote relaxation.

Scan QR Code (with camera or QR code reader) to view Relaxing Teas video.

Healthy Skin Care

Self-care also involves maintaining healthy skin. Skin Care is often neglected in the busyness of our day to day routines, however, it's important to take time to take care of your skin.

Scan QR Code (with camera or QR code reader) to view Healthy Skin Care video.

WEALTH: GIVING-SAVING-SPENDING

SCRIPTURE

Praise the Lord!
Blessed is the man who fears the Lord,
Who delights greatly in His commandments.

His descendants will be mighty on earth;
The generation of the upright will be blessed.

Wealth and riches will be in his house,
And his righteousness endures forever.

Psalms 112: 1- 3 NKJV

MISSION

Mission

To enable Christians to manage their God given wealth in a way that is pleasing to God.

INTRODUCTION

Wealth is described as **abundance of valuable material possessions or resources.** There are numerous scriptures referring to how to manage your wealth according to God's instructions and not your own. When you reach for more, but is never satisfied with your income, it is not being rich towards God. Regardless of what you have, each one should have a budget to minimize wasting resources on a plentiful supply of desirable things such as luxuries, but one must focus on how to maintain well-being and prosperity.

So, let's say that you now acquired all these possessions or resources, but you continue to work endless days and have restless nights just because it's not enough. Therefore, I recommend that you look at the parable in Luke 12:16-21 and then in Ecclesiastes 5:10-12.

The greatest trial of a good man's constancy is, when love to Jesus calls him to give up love to friends and relatives. Even when gainers by Christ, let them still expect to suffer for him, till they reach heaven. Let us learn contentment in a low state, and to watch against the love of riches in a high one. *(Luke 12:16-21 KJV)*

This scripture is communicating that money can cause a person to become selfish, greedy, and hold wealth and material things as idols before God. Preventing them from serving God whole heartedly and in true sincerity because God is not the priority, but money, wealth, and material gain is the driving force in a person's life. (Matthew 19:16-24)

Goals

If you don't know where you are going you won't know how to get there. Many people do not use a holistic approach when it comes to finances and as a result, they have investments or assets that do not align with the

goals they set for themselves. The list below can be used as a guide to create a plan for your money and even more importantly for your life!

1. Write the vision-Habakkuk 2:2
2. Be diligent-Proverbs 21:5
3. Consider your ways- Haggai 1:6-7
4. Organize your finances-1 Corinthians 14:40
5. Lending but not Borrowing-2 Kings 4:2-7
6. Pay your Taxes- Matthew 22:15-22
7. Be generous in Tithing-Malachi 3:10
8. Solving money problems- 1 Timothy 6:10
9. Leave an inheritance for children by Investing-Proverbs 13:22
10. Apply your hearts unto wisdom-Retirement Plans- Psalms 92:14
11. Creating a budget-Luke 14:28-30

'And whatsoever ye do, do it heartily, as to the Lord, and not unto men; Knowing that of the Lord ye shall receive the reward of the inheritance: for ye serve the Lord Christ. ' Colossians 3:23-24

WEALTH ASSESSMENT

This assessment was designed to give you an overview of how you are managing your finances. It will help you to think about the way you budget. It will also help you identify hindrances to you managing your finances (i.e. giving, spending, saving and investing) the way God intended. This is for your personal knowledge ONLY and can be used to make adjustments where you feel needed.

1= Strongly Agree 2=Agree   3=Neutral 4=Disagree 5= Strongly Disagree

1. I honor God with my finances by giving tithe and offering?

12345

1. I manage my finances using a weekly, bi-weekly or monthly budget?

12345

1. I try to live within my pre-planned budget?

12345

Wealth Assessment

1. I have financial resources set aside for unexpected needs (i.e. car repairs, family or home maintenance emergencies)?

1 2 3 4 5

2. I have planned for my financial future?

1 2 3 4 5

3. My goal is to live a debt free lifestyle?

1 2 3 4 5

4. I have prepared for my financial future by obtaining a 401K, IRA, ROTH IRA, or other savings plan.

1 2 3 4 5

8. Investing is based on one's financial goals and personal timeline?

1 2 3 4 5

9. I pay my bills according to my pay schedule?

1 2 3 4 5

10. When we are good stewards over our finances, God entrusts us with more?

1 2 3 4 5

11. Good stewardship over my finances includes paying my taxes.

1 2 3 4 5

12. God cares about my finances.

1 2 3 4 5

13. God will help me make the right financial decisions if I pray and ask Him.

1 2 3 4 5

14. If I pay extra payments on my mortgage or automobile loans, I will reduce the overall balance.

1 2 3 4 5

1. Everything I have belongs to God, He has just entrusted me as the steward over it.

1 2 3 4 5

GRAND TOTAL_____

Score Between 1 and 15

Good Job

Recommendations: You will need to continue managing your finances in this way. It will help you to think about the way you budget. It will also help you identify hindrances to you managing your finances the way God intended.

Score Between 16 and 30

Room for Improvement

Recommendations: You will need to make Room for Improvement managing your finances. It will also help you identify hindrances to you managing your finances (i.e. giving, spending, saving and investing) the way God intended.

Score Above 30

Need to Rethink Habits

Recommendations: You will need to rethink your habits so that you can drastically improve the way you are managing your finances. It will also help you identify hindrances to you managing your finances (i.e. giving, spending, saving and investing) the way God intended.

GIVING

Giving

There are many ways a person can give. It involves physically (serving); emotionally (listening) and materially (financially). Giving financially involves three major areas: Tithing – giving 10% of your income to the church/ministry you attend; Offering –

giving over and/or beyond the 10% percent to your church or in other ministry _____; Charity – giving to specific individual(s), causes or organizations.

Tithe – Malachi 3:10

Tithe – tenth

The Bible instructs us to tithe.

Offerings – Luke 6:38 /2 Corinthians 9:6-7

Monetary donations to a ministry over and beyond your tithe.

Charity - 1 John 3:17

Donations of time, resources and/or financially for specific causes to ministries, community or faith-based organizations.

SAVING

Saving involves putting money aside for a specified reason.

Unexpected Expenses – be prepared for the unexpected

Layoff/unemployment; natural disasters; illnesses and other adverse financial events

Educational Expenses– college savings plan for yourself or children

Ex. 529 College Savings/College Saving plans

Specific purchase – down payment for home, vehicle, etc.

Generational Inheritance – money set aside for future generations

> A good man leaves an inheritance to his children's children, ... Proverbs 13:22

Retirement – 401 K; IRA; ROTH IRA; Investments

Research to become knowledgeable about plans/options

Seek help from a trustworthy professional if you are Not financially knowledgeable

SPENDING

Household Expenses – Mortgage/Rent; Utilities; Food; Telephone:

Educational Expenses – 529 College Savings/College Saving plans

Entertainment – Eating out; concerts; sports events

Shopping – specific purposes: clothing for an event… recreational: general shopping no specified item

BUDGETING

The best way to manage your finances is to establish a budget.

Planning for your Financial Future – Creating a Budget

Habakkuk 2:2

- Write/type your budget - this allows you to see your plan and helps you to follow it

- Prepare monthly, semi-annually or annually (i.e. in advance based on your specific plan)

- List expected income and expenses

- View budget before spending

- Commit to living within your budget

- If you have excessive debt, create a debt reduction plan

- Commit to eliminating debt

- Keep plan where you can see it – this reminds you to stay focused

SAMPLE BUDGET

FAMILY MONTHLY OPERATIONAL BUDGET

DESCRIPTION

BUDGET AMOUNT: What you plan to earn and spend for the month

ACTUAL AMOUNT: What you earned and spent for the month

DIFFERENCE: Budget minus Actual equals over budget or under budget

INCOME

Earned Income:

Other Income:

Total Income:

Income Adjustment:

Sample Budget 155

Net Income:

EXPENSES

Housing Expense:

Occupancy Expense:

Telephone Expense:

Maintenance Expense:

Life Insurance Expense:

Health Insurance Expense:

Food Expense:

Entertainment Expense:

Miscellaneous Expense:

Total Expense:

Net income:

Sample Budget

Developed by Dr. Jane White

A personal budget or home budget is a finance plan that allocates future personal income towards expenses, savings and debt repayment. Past spending and personal debt are considered when creating a personal budget. There are several methods and tools available for creating, using and adjusting a personal budget. For example, jobs are an income source, while bills and rent payments are expenses.

What is Income? Earned Income: Money received from work, such as **income** from wages, salaries, fees, or the like, accruing from labor or services performed by the **earner.**

Other Income: Money received from rents, royalties, such as **investment interest, foreign exchange gains, rent income, and profit from the sale of non-inventory assets.**

Total Income: Gross family income. **The sum of all money received by an individual or organization,** including income from employment or providing services, revenue from sales, payments from pension plans, income from dividends, or other sources.

Income Adjustment: Adjustments to income are **expenses that reduce your total, or gross, income.** You enter income adjustments directly onto Form 1040 of your tax return. The amount remaining after deducting these expenses is "adjusted gross income."., such as tithing, charity, prepaid taxes, etc.

Net Income: Income left after your adjustments. Simply put, **income represents money that comes into your personal household,** usually generated as compensation in the form of a paycheck for work you have performed.

What is Expense?

Housing Expense: Your housing expense is the **total amount spent on the expenses for your home**, including your property taxes, hazard insurance and monthly mortgage payment.

Occupancy Expense: Utilities, TV, internet- costs related to occupying a space including; rent, real estate taxes, **personal** property taxes, insurance on building and contents, depreciation, and amortization **expenses**.

Telephone Expense: Home and cellular phone. The cost of **telephone** service that was used during the period shown on the income statement.

Maintenance Expense: Repairs, cleaning, security, garbage, etc. The costs incurred to bring an asset back to an earlier condition or to keep the asset operating at its present condition (as opposed to improving the asset).

Life Insurance Expense: Where the insurer promises to pay a designated beneficiary a sum of money (the benefit) in exchange for a premium, upon the death of an insured person (often the policy holder).

Health Insurance Expense: Any costs incurred in the prevention or treatment of injury or disease. Medical expenses include health and dental insurance premiums, doctor and hospital visits, co-pays, prescription and over-the-counter drugs, glasses and contacts, crutches and wheelchairs, to name a few.

Food Expense: Raw food and related supplies- **Food at home refers to the total expenditures for food from grocery stores or other food stores.** It excludes the purchase of nonfood items. Food away from home includes all meals and snacks, including tips, at fast-food, take-out, delivery and full-service restaurants, etc.

Entertainment Expense: Restaurants, movies, parties, etc. Entertainment expenses are those for any activity of the type generally considered to constitute entertainment, amusement or recreation. Examples of these activities include **sporting events, entertaining at night clubs, fishing, hunting and golf outings**.

Miscellaneous Expense: Every expected expenditure not classified. Miscellaneous Expenses include such items as **bank charges, services charges** and other minimum costs that may occur from time to time.

Total Expense: Total of all expense budgeted items. The total expense or back ratio is the minimum amounts due on your credit cards, installment loans, school loans (1% if you are deferring them unless you are doing a VA loan) child support, alimony and any back tax or other defaulted repayment arrangements you have made plus the housing expenses (Housing expenses).

Net income: Difference between Net Income and Total Expense. Simply put, **income represents money that comes into your personal household**, usually generated as compensation in the form of a paycheck for work you have performed.

Developed by Dr. Jane White

RESOURCES

- The Holy Bible, New King James Version (NKJV), Copyright 1982 Thomas Nelson.

All rights reserved.

- 9 Risk that Increases Your Risk of A Heart Attack. Emily Lockhart June 12, 2015

activebeat.com

- 10 Causes Of A Stroke. - https://1medicalnewstoday.com/

- americanmentalwellness.org

- American Psychological Association

- Anxiety and Depression Association

- arthritis.ca

- cancer.gov -

- cdc.org – Diabetes

- Harvard Health Publishing

- High blood pressure (hypertension) Mayo clinic.org

- High Cholesterol …..Mayoclinic.org.

Please go to the below links for additional information

https://www.masteringdiabetes.org/low-glycemic-fruits-for-diabetes/

https://www.dietaryguidelines.gov/sites/default/files/2019-05/2015 2020_Dietary_Guidelines.pdf

https://www.healthline.com/nutrition/best-milk-substitutes#section11

https://www.healthline.com/nutrition/soy-good-or-bad#what-is-soy

https://www.healthline.com/nutrition/9-healthy-nuts#section3

https://www.healthline.com/nutrition/6-healthiest-seeds

https://www.healthline.com/health/digestive-health/liver-cleanse

https://www.healthline.com/search?q1=colon%20cleanse

https://www.webmd.com/diet/guide/healthy-eating-nutrition

https://www.webmd.com/diet/default.htm

For budget sheets and resources on money management – www.newsprings.cc/finances

ABOUT THE AUTHOR

Dr. Jane White is a Healthcare and Business entrepreneur. She co-founded Tennessee Entrepreneur Center Incorporated, in 2018 and established Jane White, MD Ministries, Incorporated, in July 2019. She is currently a healthcare grant reviewer for the federal government and serves on a portable medicine team.

She is an appointee to the Health Education Advisory Committee for Amerigroup of Tennessee and the Faith Based Community Advisory Panel for Blue Cross Blue Shield of Tennessee. In addition, she serves as a mentor for Tennessee Promise.

Dr. White received her Bachelor of Science degree in Chemistry from Edward Waters College and her Masters in Healthcare Administration from the University of North Florida. She graduated from Washington University of Health and Science, in July 2015, earning her M.D. degree.

Dr. White's past health related positions include: Medical Director, Vice President of Operations, Chief Executive Officer, Chief Operations Officer, and Director of Operation. She has also served on various committees including the Health Council for several counties in Tennessee: Williamson; Maury, Davidson; Montgomery; Hamilton; Knox and Shelby Counties; The American College of Health Care Administrators; and was the past chapter president of The Institute of Industrial Engineers.

Dr. White was a nominee for the American College of Healthcare Executives and a 2018 recipient of the WilliamsonBusiness.Com 100 Leading African Americans.

Dr. White has a passion for serving and has always committed to enhancing her community. She served as a PTO board member for Trinity Elementary and Fred J. Page High School. She is also a former soccer coach and referee at the Williamson County Soccer Association both travel and recreation.

Dr. White desires to see people understand and embrace Spiritual Wholeness. She is a member of Shorter Chapel African Methodist Episcopal Church, in Franklin, TN. She resides in Franklin, with her husband, Dr. Ray White. They are the parents of eight children, ten grandchildren, and two great-grandchildren.

Dr. White is available to facilitate the Spiritual Wholeness Retreat. Please contact her at JaneWhite55@gmail.com for additional information.

www.ingramcontent.com/pod-product-compliance
Lightning Source LLC
LaVergne TN
LVHW051521070426
835507LV00023B/3228